NUGGETS OF AUTHENTICITY

ALICIA V. BARNES

Nuggets of Authenticity
All Rights Reserved.
Copyright © 2021 Alicia V. Barnes
v6.0

The opinions expressed in this manuscript are solely the opinions of the author and do not represent the opinions or thoughts of the publisher. The author has represented and warranted full ownership and/or legal right to publish all the materials in this book.

This book may not be reproduced, transmitted, or stored in whole or in part by any means, including graphic, electronic, or mechanical without the express written consent of the publisher except in the case of brief quotations embodied in critical articles and reviews.

Outskirts Press, Inc.
http://www.outskirtspress.com

ISBN: 978-1-9772-3460-5

Cover Photo © 2021 www.gettyimages.com. All rights reserved - used with permission.

Outskirts Press and the "OP" logo are trademarks belonging to Outskirts Press, Inc.

PRINTED IN THE UNITED STATES OF AMERICA

DEDICATION

Although I have always been loved, I have never fit in; not in my family, not in my church, not in my neighborhood, not at school, not in my profession. However, I recall with much emotion, February 22, 1986, as the first time I truly felt at home, reflecting on the words of my then Big Sister, "Welcome Home Soror." So while remaining a mystery to many, this book is dedicated to my beloved sisterhood of Alpha Kappa Alpha Sorority, Incorporated, as the space where my authentic self was discovered.

ACKNOWLEDGEMENTS

This book is a snippet of my journey. It includes insights I have learned along the way. It is a summation of my self-discovery and my course correction back to living my truth. I must therefore thank my parents Lionel "Lydie" Barnes (deceased) and Norma Barnes for loving and nurturing me, despite not truly understanding me. Special thanks to my son Nile and my daughter Nia for teaching me the art of "Listening & Hearing"—Mommy loves you so much. Finally, while inspired by God, the motivation for this work came from my sorority sister Ingrid Bough. She helped me to appreciate my workshop "Celebrating the Authentic You" as intellectual property worthy of copyright and encouraged me to transform it into this work. I am forever grateful. To God Be the Glory!

TABLE OF CONTENTS

I. SILVER—DISCOVERING THE AUTHENTIC YOU 1

II. PALLADIUM—DANGERS OF INAUTHENTIC LIVING 21

III. GOLD—BENEFITS OF AUTHENTICITY 45

IV. PLATINUM—CELEBRATING THE AUTHENTIC YOU 57

V. FINAL THOUGHTS 65

SILVER

SILVER (Ag)—Silver is one of the precious metals mentioned frequently in the Bible as a substance of value. Silver tarnishes after exposure to air (a thin layer of silver oxide forms on the surface). However, it can be polished at any time to return it to its original condition. Like Silver, exposure to the elements of life may cause us to tarnish and lose our luster. It is at these moments when we must refocus, polish, and return to our original luster.

SILVER—DISCOVERING THE AUTHENTIC YOU

Knowing and being true to who we are is the hallmark of a purposeful existence. We are exactly who we are for a reason. No one is better at being you than you. No one is more qualified to be me, than me. In fact, you are the most qualified person to be you and I am the most qualified person to be me. Let's not try to be anyone else. We are divine creations, who were created to fulfill a divine purpose. It is okay to emulate the positive characteristics we see in others. However, we must always celebrate our authenticity, because who we are is a gift from God.

SILVER—DISCOVERING THE AUTHENTIC YOU

We are exactly who and how we are for a purpose. Our race, ethnicity, physical characteristics, where we grew up, the schools we attended, the positions we've held, the mistakes we've made, are all part of our purpose, and add value to the fulfillment of our destiny. The word of God says, "All things work together for good for those of us who are called according to his purpose." Everything we have experienced may not have been good. However, once called according to God's purpose, or once we are living a purpose-driven life, our experiences—the good, the bad, and the not so good—are all a part of the master plan for our life.

SILVER—DISCOVERING THE AUTHENTIC YOU

The word "authentic" is synonymous with, authoritative, bona fide, credible, legitimate, official. While closely related to the word "genuine" which means not fake or counterfeit, authentic means conforming to fact, and therefore worthy of belief and trust. In relation to human existence, authentic living refers to knowing the person we are truly authorized to be and then legitimately functioning in our official capacity. Looking at another person's life, being envious or jealous of who they appear to be and what they appear to have, is a total waste of time; time that could be better spent focusing on developing the awesome person we were created to be. Living any other "Truth" other than our "Own" results in an illegitimate, unauthorized, unofficial existence. In a nutshell, a fake or counterfeit life; not conforming to the fact of who we were created to be, rendering us unworthy of trust or belief. It sounds horrible when expressed in these terms because truth be told, it is.

SILVER—DISCOVERING THE AUTHENTIC YOU

We must be true to ourselves or in the simplest of terms, we must live our truth. However, to live our truth, we must know who we are. We spend so much time living our less than authentic lives, because we have not taken the time to get to know ourselves. We don't really know what we like or dislike. We don't really know our strengths or our weaknesses. To truly live our best lives and be the best version of ourselves, we must take the time to get to know ourselves. Let's ask the questions. Who am I? Why am I here? Where do I want to go? How do I plan to get there? What do I want to do? How do I plan to do it?

SILVER—DISCOVERING THE AUTHENTIC YOU

In the busyness of life, we can get lost in the frenzy of doing but not being. It is important to take the time to become aware of self. We must take the time to feel ourselves feel, hear ourselves think, or simply be. So many of us have found ourselves running on empty because we have become all things to everyone with nothing left for ourselves. We spend so much time fulfilling unrealistic and unwarranted expectations at times we get lost in the shuffle or simply lose ourselves. If we are to live an authentic existence we must reconnect with ourselves. In doing so we will be able to become aware of the external stimuli that create positive or negative experiences. This awareness will lead to self-discovery and empower us to be selective in what we do, where we go, and who we associate with based on our internal response, feeling, or experience. We must pay attention to self.

SILVER—DISCOVERING THE AUTHENTIC YOU—SELF-ASSESSMENT

Self-assessment can sometimes be a scary prospect. At times it's easier to just keep on living without being aware of self. However, as divine creations we are not meant to wander aimlessly through life like driftwood. As the old adage goes, "Life is not a Spectator Sport." We must live life on purpose and with intention. In order to do so, we must determine where we are, where we want to be, and how we plan to get there. Self-assessment is an ongoing activity. It is a very important life skills tool that helps us to remain on track. When we are aware of self, through self-discovery, and we know where we are, and where we want to be, we can prioritize and streamline the affairs of our lives. We can focus on what's most important.

SILVER—DISCOVERING THE AUTHENTIC YOU—SELF DEFINITION

It is so important that we define ourselves for ourselves. It is dangerous to allow others to write our narrative or tell us who we are. So many of us have made the mistake of basing our identity on what we have, who we are with, or what we do, when in actuality it should be in the reverse. Who we are should define what we have, who we are with, and what we do. If our identity is based on external elements we simply do not know who we are nor can we recognize ourselves when stripped of those external elements. We must do an internal deep dive and determine who we are, recognizing that as divine creations we are more than enough.

SILVER—DISCOVERING THE AUTHENTIC YOU—HONESTY RATHER THAN DENIAL

Authentic living is living a life based on honesty. It's being comfortable enough in our own skin to be able to face our flaws. It's about having the courage to make the necessary adjustments to live our truth. At times we may look in the mirror and may not like what we see or who we've allowed ourselves to become. It is at these moments that we choose honesty over denial and use our power to change the image. As the Word of God states, "Why try to take the speck out of your neighbor's eye, when there is a beam in your eye." When we live in denial we see everyone's flaws but not our own. We continually make the same mistakes, refusing to take accountability for our actions. My mother once told me if you are forever in conflicts, stop to take a look at the role you are playing or have played to cause the conflict, adjust, and leave the remaining issues to God.

REFLECTIONS

_____
_____
_____
_____
_____
_____
_____
_____
_____
_____
_____
_____

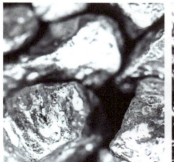   

REFLECTIONS

___
___
___
___
___
___
___
___
___
___
___
___
___

PALLADIUM

Palladium (Pd)—Discovered in 1803, Palladium is ranked amongst the precious metals. It is steelwhite in color, except in powder form, when it appears black. Palladium develops a hazy patina over time and will discolor at soldering temperatures. Palladium becomes brittle with repeated heating and cooling. Palladium can be characterized as somewhat adaptable but ultimately relatively unstable. It changes color and becomes brittle from external stimuli. Similarly, if our internal composition is not fortified, we too will become brittle when encountering life's changing temperatures.

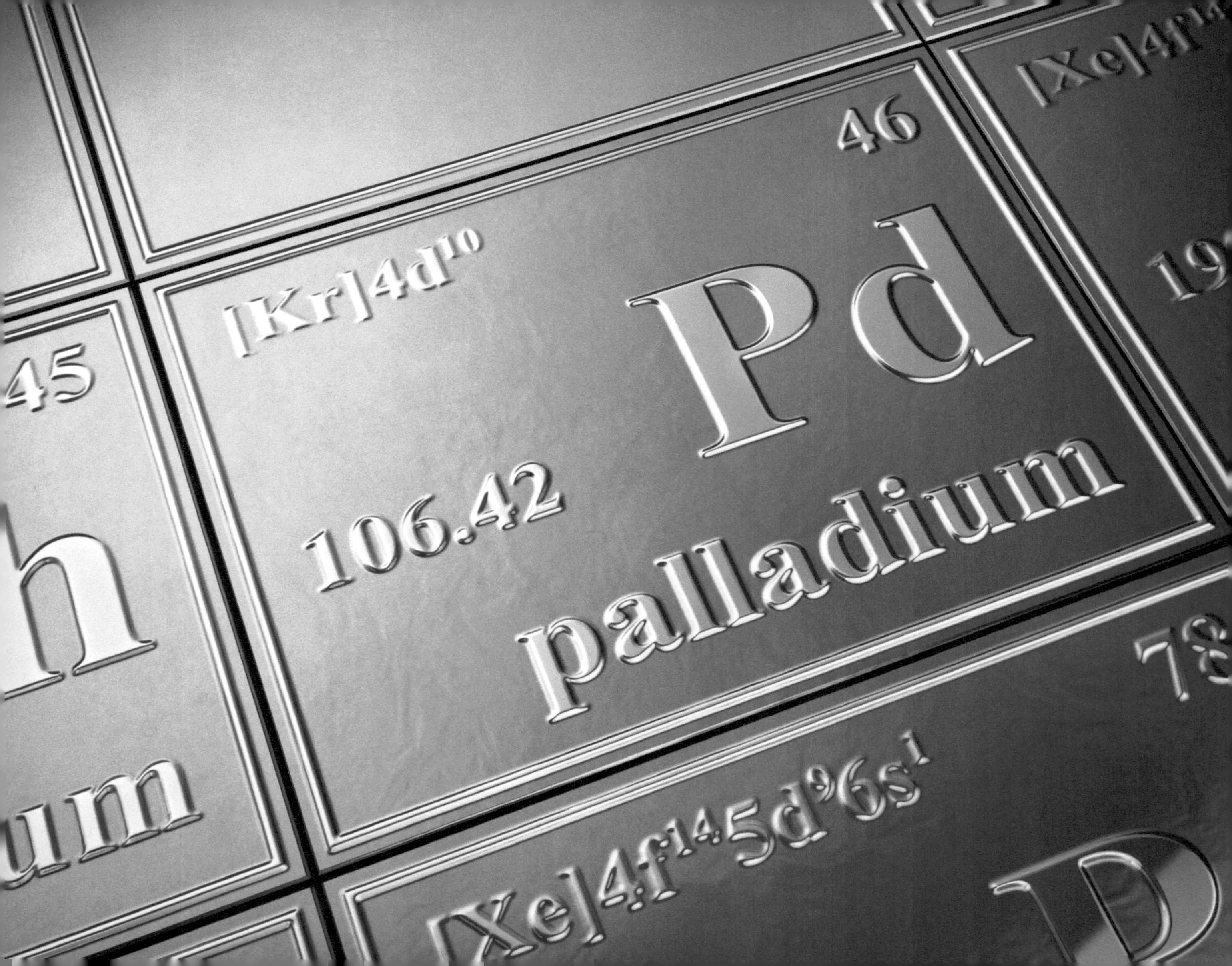
46
[Kr]4d^{10}
Pd
106.42
palladium
45
[Xe]4f^{14}5d^{9}6s^{1}

PALLADIUM—DANGERS OF INAUTHENTIC LIVING

It is very dangerous to live a life that is truly not our own. In addition to living an unauthorized, illegitimate, fictitious existence, we are denying ourselves and the world the greatness of who we were created to be. The Bible states that, "We are fearfully and wonderfully made." Why would we choose to not be who we are? We must unmask to discover and show our true essence. In doing so, we will reveal our awesomeness and the creativity that reside on the inside of us.

PALLADIUM—DANGERS OF INAUTHENTIC LIVING—IDENTITY CRISIS

Identity crises exist when we simply do not know who we are. We have not taken the time to find ourselves, and as such, we are unable to define ourselves. We depend on external stimuli and status achieved via positions, titles, and material possessions to define us. When we have these things, we are in a seemingly good place. However, when we lose them, we spiral downward as the ground begins to shift under our feet. So often we see people who appear successful succumb to suicide, addiction, substance abuse, or other forms of destructive behavior. From the outside looking in, we are shocked as we assumed that all was well, simply based on appearance. However, little did we know that the person was living a lie instead of their truth. We may fool others, but it is very hard to fool ourselves. In the quietness of our thoughts we are reminded whether we are living our truth, or not.

PALLADIUM—DANGERS OF INAUTHENTIC LIVING—NO PURPOSE

We were all created to fulfill a God-given purpose. When we are not living our authentic lives, we are not fulfilling our purpose. There is so much on the inside of us. If we don't tap into our creativity, we deny the world the blessing of our purpose. A purpose driven life fuels the passion for life. It wakes us up in the morning knowing we have something to accomplish today; someone to be a blessing to. As I wrote these words, I received a text from a college classmate thanking me for a Facebook post I made earlier in the day. The post encouraged us, "To respect ourselves enough to know that we deserve peace and to walk away from anyone or anything that disrupts it." At the reading of the post my classmate shared with me that they were in the midst of a situation at work that was disrupting their peace. My classmate was at a crossroad, in need of divine guidance. It gave me joy to know that although thousands of miles apart, my post ministered to their need and proved to be an on-time word in due season. Living a purpose driven life allows us to do the right thing at the right time. We remain in alignment with time and destiny.

PALLADIUM—DANGERS OF INAUTHENTIC LIVING—EASILY DISTRACTED—NO FOCUS—LOSS OF TIME

Life is compounding—NO Purpose, NO Plan, NO Focus. The lack of authenticity results in the lack of purpose, which results in the lack of goals. When we have no goals, we are focused on either nothing or the wrong things, and as such, are easily distracted. Everything that we see someone else doing that appears to work for them, we try. We find ourselves scurrying around from idea to idea, task to task, in a frenzy of busyness doing much but accomplishing nothing. We wake up one day and life has passed us by. We live in regret, haunted by should haves and could haves.

[Kr]4d¹⁰ — 46

Pd

106.42

palladium

PALLADIUM—DANGERS OF INAUTHENTIC LIVING—INSECURE/COMPETITIVE/INSATIABLE NEED TO MEASURE UP—

Insecurity is a natural outgrowth of inauthentic living. Feeling unsure of who we are is a stressful existence. We feel nervous and uncertain, as we are on a perpetual quest to measure up. Feelings of insecurity give rise to a competitive spirit, at best, or envy and jealousy, at worst. All negative emotions and dispositions. We want to outdo the other person (compete) or we want what the other person has (jealousy) or worst of all, we want what the other person has and we don't want them to have it (envy). The genip tree bears genips. The plum tree bears plums. Each tree knows its purpose. As silly as it sounds, consider a mango tree trying to bear plums or a genip tree trying to bear mangos. Instead each stays in their lane, and compliments the other instead of competes.

PALLADIUM—DANGERS OF INAUTHENTIC LIVING—LIFE IS LIVED FROM THE OUTSIDE IN RATHER THAN THE INSIDE OUT

When we are not living an authentic life, there is a need for constant external validation from praise, recognition, status, and material possessions. Because we are out of alignment, we need to be propped-up continually; exasperating ourselves and our loved ones. As we try to prop ourselves up with material possessions, we extend ourselves financially, buying things we can barely afford to impress folks we barely like. In essence, our motives are not pure, as our actions are self-seeking and self-serving.

MY HARD LESSON IN AUTHENTICITY

Being true to who we are at times may be one of the hardest things we do. We may have to endure the ridicule, disappointment, and disdain from family, friends, and community. Often times persons choose to, "Run your life while walking their own." The expectations of others can be a heavy burden to bear, but not living up to those expectations can be heavier. It takes courage to live your truth. I served as a Chief of Staff in the 24th and 25th Legislatures of the U.S. Virgin Islands. During my first Legislative Session, I became physically ill. I was in total shock and bewilderment at the proceedings. I vowed then that I would never run for the Senate, and I maintained that decision for more than 16 years.

MY HARD LESSON IN AUTHENTICITY

Over the course of my career, I have been asked to run for the senate by community leaders, Democratic Party bosses, family, friends, and foes. I declined each and every time. Then Hurricanes Irma and Maria devastated the U.S. Virgin Islands. My home was destroyed. The insurance companies were jerking me and everyone else around. I was frustrated for myself and others who found themselves in similar predicaments. The members of the 32nd Legislature of the U.S. Virgin Islands at the time, to me, seemed lost. It appeared as though they interpreted their role to be delivering water and providing updates on the radio. Then they passed the 'Burn Ban". A piece of Legislation that to this day still makes no sense to me. That was it! I decided to run for the senate, completely ignoring what I knew, I reacted solely by what I felt—utter frustration.

MY HARD LESSON IN AUTHENTICITY

At the writing of this book, I am less than four months away from completing my term as a freshman senator. Serving St. Croix as a member of the 33rd Legislature of the U.S. Virgin Islands will always remain an honor to me. I will continue to serve my community as I did prior to being elected. However, I find our current system of representation one that gives rise to a competitive environment rife with insecurity, as well as paranoia, and at times sabotage. This results in inefficiency and ineffectiveness. I wrestled with my decision for months, but knew deep down inside what it would be. The thought of campaigning and asking my constituents to vote for me, via a flawed system, with the expectation that I could truly improve their quality of life in earnest, was conflicting. I simply could not, knowing what I know, and experiencing what I experienced. My decision to not seek reelection set off a whirlwind of emotions, scrutiny, and speculation from the public that remains very difficult to comprehend and painful to experience. Never did I anticipate such a volatile and at times explosive reaction.

MY HARD LESSON IN AUTHENTICITY

The experience gave me insight into the "heart of man"; illuminating the words of Abraham Lincoln, "If you want to know a man's true character, give him power." However, I remain at peace with my decision, knowing that the course correction was necessary to realign and return to my destined path. When you are out of alignment there is turmoil and confusion, which I experienced from day one after being elected. Unintended consequences of damaged relationships more than anything I had ever experienced in a lifetime occurred within my first year as a senator; by far the worst experience of my professional career. Truly a hard lesson in authenticity and the dangers of misalignment. Being proud of my legislative record, my only regret is the broken relationships which I am hopeful and prayerful will mend and heal with time.

REFLECTIONS

_____
_____
_____
_____
_____
_____
_____
_____
_____
_____
_____
_____

REFLECTIONS

GOLD

GOLD (Au)—Gold is a highly sought-after rare precious metal. For many centuries Gold has been used for money, jewelry and ornamentation symbolizing wealth and prosperity. In the Bible, Gold is considered holy and set apart. It is the only precious metal mentioned before the "Fall of Man". When exposed to heat, Gold is purified and strengthened. "But HE knows the way I take. When HE has tried me, I shall come forth as Gold"—Job 23:10. Like Gold, when exposed to life's fiery trials we will be purified; revealing the strength of our authentic selves.

GOLD—BENEFITS OF AUTHENTICITY

"You shouldn't need an escape from your life."—TK Petersen, Co-founder and CFO of The Gathering Spot. What I thought would be a routine interview with one of my son's childhood friends turned into a lesson in authentic living as TK Petersen spoke of his journey from being an up and coming corporate executive to becoming an entrepreneur. He spoke of the concern from some members of his family as he turned down job offers and opportunities to pursue his dream. Later that day I received a call from one of my best friends stating that the interview moved her to tears as she reflected on her own choices and the expectations she was imposing on her child, instead of listening to her child's voice.

GOLD—BENEFITS OF AUTHENTICITY

This in turn caused me to reflect on my son, Nile, and his journey to authenticity. The unfair expectations I imposed on him and his strength to push back and push on despite the doubters. When persons do not understand your life of truth they create their own narrative originating from their limited thinking. So, while most of my son's peers live in a virtual social media world, my son has chosen to live his truth in the real world with organic relationships and business associates. My son's journey is a testament to his God-given strength and the power of love from family and community. His journey ushered him into a place of peace knowing he is on his destined path.

GOLD—BENEFITS OF AUTHENTICITY

I reflect also on my niece, Dr. Tramaine Creighton, who was cautioned against choosing veterinary school instead of medical school. Tramaine, who was born with a love for animals, tuned out the voices of the naysayers and well-intentioned bystanders to pursue her passion. Finally, my daughter Nia, who is pursuing a career in Naturopathic Medicine. She too is experiencing the looks of puzzlement and concern when explaining her career choice. As the steward entrusted by God to be her mother, I am blessed to aid her in navigating her course. I am still in awe that at the tender age of 16, Nia discovered her purpose. Nile, Nia, Tramaine, and TK possess the courage to live their truth; in doing so they will fulfill their purpose and destiny.

GOLD—BENEFITS OF AUTHENTICITY

Consider our elders who transition peacefully. Because they have lived a full life and maximized time, they are prepared to hear, "Well done my good and faithful servant,"—because they know they,—"Ran THEIR Race and finished THEIR Course," and not someone else's. They lived an authentic life and fulfilled their purpose. When I served as Energy Director, I received an unscheduled visit from a gentleman by the name of James Maynard from Harlem. Although unscheduled, I was curious to meet him because my mother's maiden name is Maynard. The moment I laid eyes on him I knew he was family. He looked very much like my mother. As he proceeded to tell me about his studies, at the time he was a college professor, I could not contain myself. I interrupted him and asked him the origin of his last name. He then told me that in the early 1900's his grandfather left Nevis and traveled to Harlem. He further explained that he had been trying unsuccessfully to find his Nevisian family. I asked him his grandfather's name and he said, Joseph. I got goosebumps because in my mother's family the names James, Charles and Joseph are recurring from generation to generation. I immediately called my mother who confirmed by stating, "In the early 1900's Papa had a brother, Uncle Joe, who left on the steamship to New York and never came back." At that point, I looked at James Maynard and told him that he had just found his Nevisian family. Soon thereafter, in 1997, the Maynard Family held its first reunion in Nevis. James Maynard and the entire Maynard Clan from Harlem, New York traveled to Nevis and met their Caribbean-family. We remain connected to this day. Shortly after our 1997 reunion, my cousin James Maynard transitioned. As a result of both James and I being in alignment with our purpose and destiny, we were in the right place at the right time. This allowed for the reconnection of members of the Maynard family throughout the Caribbean diaspora. I was honored to represent the Caribbean Maynard Clan at James' funeral in Harlem.

REFLECTIONS

_____
_____
_____
_____
_____
_____
_____
_____
_____
_____
_____
_____

REFLECTIONS

PLATINUM

Platinum (Pt)—Platinum is more precious than Gold, it is a very strong dense metal that never corrodes. In its purest form, it is harder than gold and silver. It is a rare greyish white metal. Ten tons of ore have to be mined to produce one ounce of platinum. Like Platinum, we are strong, rare, and more precious than Gold.

PLATINUM—CELEBRATING THE AUTHENTIC YOU

The Benefits of Authentic Living are infinite. We live a life of purpose and passion. We know who we are, and why we are here. This gives us the desire to awake every morning with excitement and anticipation because we have a vision for our lives and our future. We wake up each day excited as we are truly on a mission. We live life strategically and not emotionally, focusing on our dreams and goals. Our focus minimizes distractions and streamlines our lives. We know what activities will move us closer to achieving our vision and what activities will move us farther away. We maximize time by minimizing distractions. We are not moved by what others are doing or what others have. There is no need to compete, as we only seek to compliment. This allows us to live life from the inside out and not the outside in. Authentic living eliminates insecurity, because we are living the life we are authorized to live. We are not trespassing on another person's life.

PLATINUM—CELEBRATING THE AUTHENTIC YOU

We are living our own life, on our own terms, and we are authorized to do so. We are validated by an internal compass. Our vision is the barometer utilized to evaluate our actions and inactions. It provides the perspective needed to ensure our motives are pure and intentions honest and aligned with our purpose. We can look back over our lives and recall moments when we were truly "out of sorts". We were off kilter. Something just was not right. Those are the moments our internal compass is trying to tell us that we need a course correction. That we are on the wrong path. We are out of our lane at best or heading in the wrong direction at worst.

PLATINUM—CELEBRATING THE AUTHENTIC YOU

When we are living authentic lives, we get the nudge needed to make the course correction to get back on track or change direction. This is so very important to fulfilling our destiny. If we are not where we are supposed to be, doing what we are supposed to be doing, we are unable to fulfill our purpose. However, like my cousin James Maynard, when we are where we are supposed to be, doing what we are supposed to be doing, we will make a positive and lasting impact on society. In doing so at the end of our journey we hear the words, "Well done my good and faithful servant, enter into the joys of heaven."

FINAL THOUGHTS

So, in the final analysis, the conclusion of the matter is when we embrace our authenticity, we live the life we were destined to live. We become strategically positioned to be blessed and to bless others in return. We navigate life as bona fide officials who are duly authorized to legitimately and passionately pursue our purpose. Let's go forth, Celebrating Our Authenticity and LIVE OUR BEST LIFE NOW!

REFLECTIONS

_____
_____
_____
_____
_____
_____
_____
_____
_____
_____
_____
_____
_____

REFLECTIONS

CPSIA information can be obtained
at www.ICGtesting.com
Printed in the USA
LVHW070453210221
679526LV00003B/47